Waves of Creativity

LIZ PERKINS

WAVES OF CREATIVITY

Liz Perkins

ISBN: 978-1-66783-409-2

Waves of Creativity Book Index

Gathering Clouds

Have you ever had one of those perplexing days?
Totally discombobulated; nothing going your way.
I found a solution, something I discovered
Quite by chance one day as clouds gathered.

Glancing up to the sky I saw formations,
Of cirrus and stratus clouds.
Shapes varying perspectives and differing sizes
White, fluffy cumulus evolving; metamorphosis.

At first just a head appeared
That grew into a rabbit, long eared.
Now a fiery dragon truly feared.
Then suddenly, "puff", just like that
All dispersed and disappeared.

As did those worries, rattling round in my head.
What concerns? For they are now totally fled
And my mind once again, calm,
Fueled with positivity instead.

Grandad's Boat

At the end of the dock the small boat awaits,
A floating heaven for all and their mates.
Tenderly cared for over long time,
Painted and varnished and spared not a dime.

That little boat, oh what adventures it has seen.
Here for years but unknown exactly where it has been.
Many a person has sat and fished
Or rowed and sculled as much as they wished.

It's been swum from and dived from
Even left out to drift.
Enjoyed by so many:
Like life, it's a gift.

Medusa Jellyfish

What mystical, magical, medusa creatures
these jellyfish are.

Discovered long ago in olden times
In diverse temperatures, warm or cold climes.
Living in swarms beneath the waves
Swimming in currents and carried by tides
Found throughout in seas and oceans worldwide.
Some can produce their own light from inside
And in the deep waters show an internal glow
With free swimming tentacles streaming below.

What mystical, magical, medusa creatures
these jellyfish are.

Nautilus Shells

Swirls and twirls that catch the light
Shining, pearly, glistening bright.
Shells like these are a pure delight
To heighten our minds and bring thoughts to excite.

What lived in this? Where did it go?
Was it safe in its home or did it outgrow
This cosy, curly haven.

I guess it's another tale of the seas
Another of life's mysteries
To remain unsolved
Of how shells evolved.

No Boundaries

Do you know where you can go
For total relaxation?
No boundaries or fences
Just pure liberation.

Enter a time capsule
Of mental elation
Freedom of mind
For your own creation.

Take your bike to the beach
And go for a ride.
Pedal through the puddles
Of the ebbing tide.

With the sun on your face
And wind through your hair
Absorb the sound, the smell
And tang of the fresh salty air.

Now you know where you can go!
Come with me if you dare.
Come with me to the beach
That beach over there.

Ocean Waves

White caps and hues of blues and greens
As far as the eye can see
All the way to the edge of the earth,
That's infinity.

There's a sand bar out there
So, swimmers beware of
The riptides that lurk beneath.
They grab you and swirl you and carry you far
Far from the beaches reach.

The cresting waves break like a serpent's head
As they crash and cascade on the shore
With a hunger that is perpetually fed
By the currents and tides that draw.

Foam on foam they pulse on the land
with noise in your ears like a roar
Leaving white lacey tendrils tickling the sand
As they then recede once more.

The ever-changing ocean repeats itself
Over and over again
Into the shore then out to sea
Its energy to sustain.

Pathway to Paradise

Following the pathway to paradise
Is really a dream to come true
It is all one could wish for
To arrive and see that view.

The seagrass and palms
Frame each side of the way
As we head on down to the sea.
Our excitement rising fervently
Oh! what a day this will be.

The smell of salt air, the feel of the sand
The calls of the gulls and the terns.
Our hearts skip a beat
We've arrived, what a treat.
Then "Cream Up" to prevent sunburns.

Yes, this is the haven for family fun
To swim or frolic in the sand.
Or maybe just lounge and enjoy the day
The sights and sounds and then just say
"Thank you" in a gargantuan way.

Pillars of Time

Pillars of time withstand the continual
tides' flow and ebb
But life changes daily, it's complicated
just like an intricate web.
So, be strong, stand tall and follow your dreams
Whatever they may be.
Choose the path towards a happy life
That's stress and trouble free.

Sanderlings at the Shore

So quick and fine those tiny legs
Run back and forth like clockwork pegs
Along the sandy shore.

They scoot and scoop through water and sand
For any crustacean they can land.
They pick with their beaks
Where the sand and sea meets;
Following the tide line in and out.
Quick 'kip' their call is heard all about.

Why don't they trip when their beaks touch the ground?
Instead, they just simply spin around
And continue their everlasting sound.
Skipping the waves
Their lives to save
Those quick trotting Sanderlings

Sea-life

Seahorses, turtles and nautilus shells
Blue crab and lobster too.
These beautiful creatures are all to be found
Under the sea so blue.

They all play their part in their own special way
For the balance of life in the sea.
Some swimming or floating or nesting in sand
Each lifestyle a unique specialty.

Sea life is something that needs total protection
Pollution resolved by early detection
Preserve sands and coral reefs to continue to grow
To maintain clean oceans both above and below.

"Skippy" the Seahorse

In shallow coastal waters, reefs and sea grass beds
You'll find the hippocampus with his equine horse-like head.

He's such a pretty fellow, very cute and loveable
But he's a pretty poor swimmer as his fin is very small.
With a toothless mouth and body of rings of bony plates
The seahorse is unique as he only has one mate.

He jigs about up, down, front, back and to the side
And uses his prehensile tail, clinging on to catch a ride.
Wouldn't you like to have a ride on "Skippy" through the seas
Or even in the shallowness of coastal estuaries.

Close your eyes and dream of this as you drift off to sleep
A fun idea beneath the sea great memories to keep

Sunrise Sailing

The weekend is here
It's time to go – "Anchor A'weigh"
Haul the sails – "lee ho".

Leaving the creek, adventure awaits.
Escape the rush, the City and the dates.
Appointments forgotten
Deadline? How? What? When?
Start to relax, we're sailing again.

The sun is up. The mist is low.
Droplets glisten, on the tender in tow.
The channel buoys are now in sight
If we make good time
We'll drop anchor tonight!

Work is Done

Sit back, relax
All work is done.
Take time for oneself
To lounge in the sun.

Use osmosis, absorb aromas
And vistas of the sea
Conjuring up an inner sense
Of total tranquility.

Dreams for tomorrow
Or memories to mind returned
This valuable time
Has been duly earned.

Sit back, relax
All work is done
Precious moments like this
Are second to none.

Liz (Elizabeth) Perkins

I am from Whitstable, Kent, a coastal fishing town in SE England and known as Liz to my family and friends. My husband, Alan and I came to the USA in 1997 having accepted an offer to work together and are very happy that we accomplished our mission. We became US Citizens in 2010 and are now living our retirement dream in The Villages, Florida.

My parents were a major influence in my life. My father, with his strong positive attitude, always supported and encouraged me. I believe he inspired my interest in poetry, he often wrote poetry for my mother and it was my mother that instilled in me her mantra: "never give up on whatever you do". She was a widow for 40 years and had an incredible life before passing at age 101.

Alan, my husband, is my mainstay and my hero. Together we make an amazing team. My thanks and appreciation go to him for his "stickability" and support for all the crazy ideas I come up with. We are very blessed to have Becky and Ricky, our daughter and son-in-law with Madison, our amazing, lovely granddaughter living in Charleston, SC. Family means the world to us.

Sincere thanks go to Alan, Becky Gerry our daughter, Alan's brother Mike Perkins and Alan's friend Jim Kelly for the wonderful photos and pictures that were taken by this artistic group and edited by Becky which helped to make this book "Waves of Creativity" possible. Also thanks go to my new friend Mary Ellen Taylor who, after a synchronistic meeting, invited me to write poems supporting her artwork for a joint book venture we produced and thus resulting in the enthusiasm to produce this book.